STRAIN your BRAIN
QUESTION & ANSWER
GAME BOOK 4

D0950218

Published by Playmore Inc., Publishers and
Waldman Publishing Corp., New York, New York

The Playmore/Waldman ® is a registered
trademark of Playmore Inc., Publishers and
Waldman Publishing Corp., New York, New York

The Playmore Waldman logo is a trademark
owned by Playmore Inc., Publishers and
Waldman Publishing Corp., New York, New York

Copyright © MMI Playmore Inc., Publishers and
Waldman Publishing Corp., New York, New York

All rights reserved. No part of this book may be
reproduced in any form or any media without the
express written permission of the publishers.

Printed in Canada

Game #1

1. Which isn't a baby bird?
a) chick   b) nestling
c) fledgling   d) hen

2. Which is the first book of the Hebrew Bible?
a) Genesis   b) Numbers
c) Leviticus   d) Exodus

3. What was Humpty Dumpty?
a) a loaf of bread   b) a glass of milk
c) an egg   d) a king

4. Which isn't found on a farm?
a) plow   b) combine
c) harpoon   d) harvester

5. Which word doesn't give you chills?
a) glacier   b) icicle
c) floe   d) dew

6. What sound does a mule or donkey make?
a) growl   b) heehaw
c) purr   d) bark

7. Mutton comes from which animal?
a) cow   b) buffalo
c) sheep   d) hog

8. What is the opposite of acquire?
a) forfeit   b) get
c) gain   d) secure

9. What is a nanny?
a) a goat or horse   b) a goat or nursemaid
c) a horse or nursemaid   d) a handkerchief

10. What is the opposite of actual?
a) sure-enough   b) genuine
c) imaginary   d) real

Game #2

1. When is the season of holly and mistletoe?
a) Easter　　　　　　b) Thanksgiving
c) Christmas　　　　d) Election Day

2. What is the opposite of add?
a) total　　　　　　b) subtract
c) attach　　　　　d) increase

3. What is the seed of an oak?
a) pecan　　　　　　b) nutmeg
c) acorn　　　　　　d) walnut

4. What is a female sheep?
a) jenny   b) mare
c) ewe   d) hen

5. Which is an owl call?
a) chirp   b) peep
c) whistle   d) hoot

6. What's the same as being ill-at-ease?
a) calm   b) collected
c) cool   d) anxious

7. What is the fruit of the pine called?
a) acorn   b) filbert
c) cone   d) pecan

8. What is another name for a country road?

a) thruway

b) highway

c) lane

d) autobahn

9. Which isn't one of Santa Claus's reindeer?

a) Vixen

b) Lightning

c) Comet

d) Dasher

10. What's the same as come into sight?

a) vanish

b) disappear

c) appear

d) depart

Game #3

1. What sound does a snake make?
a) whistle   b) bark
c) chirp   d) hiss

2. In which city is the Kremlin?
a) St. Petersburg   b) Warsaw
c) Moscow   d) Kiev

3. What's another word for mop?
a) swab   b) swaddle
c) swag   d) swack

4. What's the same as help?
a) assist
b) impede
c) block
d) hamper

5. Which is not a Norse country?
a) Iceland
b) Sweden
c) Estonia
d) Denmark

6. Which is not a moor?
a) forest
b) fen
c) bog
d) swamp

7. Which tool is not used for cutting?
a) scalpel
b) scythe
c) stapler
d) scissors

8. Which musical instrument is like a marimba?
a) xylophone   b) harp
c) harmonica   d) oboe

9. Which game doesn't use a table?
a) pool   b) Ping-Pong
c) billiards   d) hopscotch

10. What's the opposite of authentic?
a) true   b) genuine
c) spurious   d) real

Game #4

1. Where does a subway train get its power from?
a) overhead line
b) third rail
c) gasoline engine
d) steam engine

2. Which is the central section of an airplane?
a) pontoon
b) vertical fin
c) fuselage
d) cockpit

3. What is a small-size newspaper called?
a) comic book
b) paperback
c) magazine
d) tabloid

4. What kind of knot is used to tie a man's tie?
a) granny
b) Windsor knot
c) bow
d) square knot

5. What do you call the sweater with a high, turned-down collar?
a) crew neck
b) turtleneck
c) boat neck
d) v-neck

6. Which is not another word for thin?
a) reedy
b) lanky
c) hefty
d) skinny

7. Which isn't used for cleaning?
a) brush
b) broom
c) mop
d) scythe

8. Which doesn't measure distance?
a) yard   b) mile
c) kilometer   d) ton

9. Which word does not refer to evening?
a) dusk   b) nightfall
c) first light   d) twilight

10. Which state is not on the Pacific coast?
a) Washington   b) California
c) Georgia   d) Oregon

Game #5

1. What, basically, is a collie?
a) a lapdog
b) a sheepdog
c) a bird dog
d) a watchdog

2. What is a sheepskin?
a) a woolen shirt
b) a diploma
c) a heavy sweater
d) scraps of wool

3. What's another word for singing softly with closed lips?
a) chanting
b) humming
c) yodeling
d) warbling

4. What are moccasins?
a) birds & snakes   b) birds & shoes
c) shoes & snakes   d) imitations & errors

5. Complete the proverb: "When the cat's away, the mice will —"
a) eat a lot of cheese   b) purr
c) play   d) watch TV

6. Where are Waikiki Beach and Pearl Harbor?
a) North Dakota   b) Kansas
c) Vermont   d) Hawaii

7. In which city do you celebrate Mardi Gras in the French Quarter?
a) Detroit   b) Galveston
c) Cincinnati   d) New Orleans

8. Which of the following is used in an orchestra?
a) cymbal
b) symbol
c) simpleton
d) sample

9. Which one is no place to get food?
a) a restaurant
b) a luncheonette
c) a diner
d) a launch pad

10. What is the seed of an apple usually called?
a) pip
b) stone
c) kernel
d) pod

Game #6

1. In the *Harry Potter* books, who isn't a wizard?
a) a mumbler
b) a bumbler
c) a muggle
d) a fumbler

2. Who wrote *Little Women*?
a) Harriet Beecher Stowe
b) Louisa May Alcott
c) Julia Ward Howe
d) Judy Blume

3. Which word is not used in golfing?
a) divot
b) eagle
c) birdie
d) inning

4. Who plays Will Smith's partner in the movie *Men in Black*?
a) Tommy Lee Jones   b) Rip Torn
c) Vincent D'Onofrio   d) Tony Shalhoub

5. Which creature doesn't build a nest?
a) wasp   b) ant
c) dog   d) bird

6. Who plays Sally Solomon on *3rd Rock from the Sun*?
a) Kristen Johnston   b) Jane Curtin
c) Alison Sweeney   d) Rosie O'Donnell

7. What is a frankfurter?
a) a small dog   b) a hot dog
c) a dog biscuit   d) a dachshund

8. The bald-headed captain of the Starship Enterprise is Jean-Luc _____

a) Kirk   b) Picard

c) Pickle   d) Picadilly

9. Which one isn't a horn?

a) bugle   b) trumpet

c) clarinet   d) trombone

10. What is the title for the chief on-air person of television news?

a) news anchor   b) cameraman

c) company president   d) producer

Game #7

1. What is TNT?
a) a Swedish rock group   b) an explosive
c) a government agency   d) an insecticide

2. Which tool doesn't grip?
a) vise   b) pincers
c) screwdriver   d) tweezers

3. What is the end car of a train called?
a) metro   b) dining car
c) caboose   d) freight car

4. Which tree does not bear cones?
a) fir   b) spruce
c) oak   d) larch

5. What kind of railroad is underground?
a) scenic   b) subway
c) elevated   d) trans-continental

6. Which one is not a term used at sea?
a) ahoy   b) avast
c) belay   d) giddyap

7. Who is not a Broadway star?
a) lead   b) heroine
c) stand-in   d) hero

8. What is another name for Japan?

a) Saipan   b) Taipei

c) Nippon   d) Canton

9. Which one is not a martial art?

a) karate   b) karma

c) judo   d) kung fu

10. What are terrapins and tortoises?

a) lizards   b) snakes

c) reptiles   d) amphibians

Game #8

1. Who is the Norse god of thunder?
a) Odin   b) Loki
c) Baldar   d) Thor

2. How many units are there in threescore?
a) three   b) three hundred
c) thirty   d) sixty

3. What is a midge?
a) a short person   b) an insect
c) an Annapolis student   d) an itch

4. Which isn't a military storehouse?

a) commissary

b) cache

c) depot

d) arsenal

5. What is the same as a slap in the face?

a) insult

b) honor

c) compliment

d) flattery

6. What's the opposite of without exception?

a) never

b) in every case

c) constantly

d) forever

7. Which isn't a melon?

a) honeydew

b) cantaloupe

c) papaya

d) pomegranate

8. Which river is featured in the book *Huckleberry Finn*?

a) Amazon   b) Rio Grande
c) Mississippi   d) Potomac

9. Which is not a Japanese dish?

a) sashimi   b) teriyakii
c) sushi   d) haggis

10. What is the capital of Maryland?

a) Baltimore   b) Hagerstown
c) Annapolis   d) Frederick

Game #9

1. What is the name of tennis player Serena Williams' sister?
a) Venus
b) Vanessa
c) Victoria
d) Vera

2. Which is a tourist resort in Idaho?
a) Spring Valley
b) Silicon Valley
c) Sun Valley
d) Valley of the Moon

3. Where is The Land of Lincoln?
a) Kentucky
b) Illinois
c) Missouri
d) Tennessee

4. Which word doesn't mean legal?
a) legitimate   b) licit
c) official   d) unlawful

5. Which word isn't a Native American term?
a) papoose   b) wampum
c) succotash   d) goulash

6. What is another word for apple juice?
a) sap   b) milk
c) perry   d) cider

7. Who loved Juliet?
a) Capulet   b) Hector
c) Romeo   d) Antony

8. What is the capital of Kansas?
a) Kansas City   b) Topeka
c) Wichita   d) Abalone

9. What is the name of Gilbert & Sullivan's operetta about Japan?
a) *HMS Pinafore*   b) *Iolanthe*
c) *The Mikado*   d) *Ruddigore*

10. What describes a humane person?
a) watchful   b) kind
c) stingy   d) bossy

Game #10

1. Which one is not the chief officer of a ship?
a) master
b) skipper
c) captain
d) helmsman

2. Who does the bullfighter face in the ring?
a) a muleta
b) el toro
c) a toreador
d) a matador

3. Which is not a branch of mathematics?
a) algebra
b) trigonometry
c) rhetoric
d) arithmetic

4. Which was the sister ship of the Pilgrims' vessel, *Speedwell?*
a) *Independence*   b) *Constitution*
c) *Mayflower*   d) *Merrimac*

5. Which one is not a novice?
a) rookie   b) neophyte
c) veteran   d) apprentice

6. What state is Walden Pond in?
a) Maine   b) Vermont
c) New Hampshire   d) Massachusetts

7. Who is not a patriarch of the Bible?
a) Abraham   b) Isaac
c) Jacob   d) Solomon

8. Which is a Mexican blanket?
a) tamale   b) perro
c) serape   d) adobe

9. What is another word for noon?
a) midday   b) daybreak
c) evening   d) dusk

10. A Green Beret is a member of which elite fighting unit?
a) Rangers   b) Marines
c) Special Forces   d) Navy Seals

Game #11

1. What is a minaret?
a) a small excavation b) a tower
c) a type of fly   d) a torpedo

2. Which mineral doesn't burn?
a) anthracite   b) bitumen
c) asbestos   d) lignite

3. Which mineral is used in pencils?
a) lead   b) graphite
c) copper   d) platinum

4. What is the capital of Minnesota?
a) Minneapolis   b) Duluth
c) Rochester   d) St. Paul

5. Who was the sister of Moses and Aaron?
a) Deborah   b) Sarah
c) Miriam   d) Ruth

6. Which one is not a Mountain State?
a) Kansas   b) Utah
c) Montana   d) Idaho

7. What is a group of four musicians called?
a) fourth   b) forum
c) quartet   d) quart

8. Which is an important product of Mississippi?
a) codfish
b) coal
c) cotton
d) coffee

9. What is another word for military base?
a) foxhole
b) commissary
c) encampment
d) echelon

10. Which one is the Show Me State?
a) New York
b) California
c) Florida
d) Missouri

Game #12

1. What was Moby Dick?
a) a white whale   b) a pirate captain
c) a great white shark   d) a flying horse

2. What is espresso?
a) a shoe   b) a train
c) a snake   d) a type of coffee

3. What is a molar?
a) a tooth   b) a skin blemish
c) a kind of syrup   d) a burrowing animal

4. Movie actress Grace Kelly became princess of which country?
a) Mauritania
b) Moldavia
c) Morocco
d) Monaco

5. What is a mortarboard?
a) a plank of putty
b) a ship's cannon
c) a graduate's hat
d) a concrete wall

6. Which isn't a dragonfly?
a) mosquito hawk
b) praying mantis
c) darning needle
d) snake doctor

7. Which musical instrument doesn't use a keyboard?
a) piano
b) organ
c) trombone
d) accordion

8. Benito Mussolini was dictator of what country?
a) Rumania
b) Spain
c) Portugal
d) Italy

9. A nag is what kind of animal?
a) old horse
b) old dog
c) old ox
d) old goat

10. What's another way of referring to a maiden name?
a) nickname
b) sobriquet
c) nee
d) pen name

Game #13

1. Naples is a city in which country?
a) Spain   b) Greece
c) Italy   d) France

2. What is a nautical mile?
a) a knot   b) a beam
c) a fathom   d) a mast

3. Which is a navigator?
a) a dancer   b) a chef
c) a flyer   d) a barber

4. Who is not a navy officer?
a) admiral
b) commodore
c) corporal
d) captain

5. Which character is not in *Peter Pan*?
a) Tinker Bell
b) Wendy
c) Long John Silver
d) Tiger Lily

6. Which isn't a magical term?
a) jeepers creepers
b) presto
c) abracadabra
d) sesame

7. Which is not a form of necktie?
a) four-in-hand
b) Windsor
c) cravat
d) dickie

8. What is the hole in a needle called?
a) a brad　　　　　b) an eye
c) a stylus　　　　d) a nail

9. Which isn't a form of needlework?
a) crocheting　　　b) riveting
c) sewing　　　　　d) embroidery

10. The Himalayas are associated with which country?
a) Paraguay　　　　b) Austria
c) Nepal　　　　　d) Vietnam

Game #14

1. Hank, Whitney, Pilar and Tabitha are characters in which soap opera?
a) *General Hospital*   b) *Guiding Light*
c) *One Life to Live*   d) *Passions*

2. Neptune was a legendary god of what domain?
a) the sea   b) the mountains
c) the air   d) the fields

3. What is the capital of Scotland?
a) Inverness   b) Aberdeen
c) Dundee   d) Edinburgh

4. Which isn't used in gardening?
a) hoe   b) rake
c) spatula   d) spade

5. Which one was not a homesteader?
a) nester   b) settler
c) mountain man   d) Sooner

6. What is an eagle's nest?
a) web   b) aerie
c) den   d) lair

7. What is the limb of a seal called?
a) arm   b) leg
c) flipper   d) fin

8. What is another name for a jukebox?
a) pin ball machine   b) nickelodeon
c) penny arcade   d) slot machine

9. Where was Noah's Ark said to have landed?
a) Ararat   b) Gibraltar
c) Ankara   d) Atlantis

10. Which one is not a nobleman?
a) marquis   b) count
c) serf   d) baron

Game #15

1. Which is not the name of a Norse god?
a) Mars   b) Thor
c) Odin   d) Balder

2. What is sleet?
a) mud   b) lava
c) snow and rain   d) heavy rain

3. Who is not a college official?
a) dean   b) bursar
c) adjutant   d) chancellor

4. What is a wildcatter?
a) lion hunter
b) oil prospector
c) zoo doctor
d) a Jaguar car driver

5. What is giving ten percent of one's income to good works called?
a) teething
b) tilting
c) tithing
d) trothing

6. What are opossums and kangaroos?
a) birds
b) marsupials
c) predators
d) beasts of burden

7. Which is not an orange?
a) Jaffa
b) Valencia
c) Seville
d) Persian

8. Where would you mostly likely find an outpost?
a) frontier
b) hometown
c) downtown
d) next door

9. Which animal is not a pachyderm?
a) elephant
b) hippopotamus
c) wildebeest
d) rhinoceros

10. Which is used in painting?
a) gurney
b) hoist
c) palette
d) lathe

Game #16

1. What is the capital of Pakistan?
a) Karachi
b) Islamabad
c) Lahore
d) Hyderabad

2. What is a bearcat?
a) badger
b) wolverine
c) panda
d) cougar

3. *Maggio* is May in which language?
a) Turkish
b) Irish
c) Italian
d) Norwegian

4. Which pants are made of leather?
a) jeans   b) slacks
c) overalls   d) chaps

5. Who wasn't put into the furnace of Babylon?
a) Abednego   b) Meshach
c) Samson   d) Shadrach

6. Which isn't gummed paper?
a) a label   b) a stub
c) a stamp   d) a sticker

7. Where is Notre Dame Cathedral?
a) Berlin   b) London
c) Madrid   d) Paris

8. What is a first-time performance called?
a) matinee
b) debut
c) solo
d) concert

9. What is another word for an eighty-year-old person?
a) octogenarian
b) septuagenarian
c) Methuselah
d) nonagenarian

10. Which best defines a Good Samaritan?
a) charitable
b) cheery
c) ambitious
d) energetic

Game #17

1. What do penguins or seals call home?
a) a nest   b) a den
c) a lair   d) a rookery

2. Which one is not wealthy?
a) nabob   b) millionaire
c) plutocrat   d) indigent

3. Which isn't a wrestling hold?
a) mat   b) nelson
c) headlock   d) scissors

4. How many years in a millennium?
a) one hundred b) one million
c) one thousand d) ten thousand

5. Who is not a commissioned officer?
a) general b) major
c) chief petty officer d) colonel

6. Which is not a Navy vessel?
a) catamaran b) cruiser
c) submarine d) destroyer

7. What is a Jolly Roger?
a) happy TV host b) a dessert
c) a pirate flag d) a playful dog

8. What is a southpaw?
a) left-handed person   b) a cat's-foot
c) a Southern dessert   d) a heavy shoe

9. Which isn't a plaid pattern?
a) tartan   b) checkered
c) star-spangled   d) crossbarred

10. Which is the Red Planet?
a) Saturn   b) Jupiter
c) Mars   d) Pluto

Game #18

1. What sound do wolves make?
a) purr   b) neigh
c) chirp   d) howl

2. What is an arboreal plant?
a) a shrub   b) a hedge
c) a vine   d) a tree

3. Who was Robin Hood's sweetheart?
a) Guinevere   b) Becky Sharp
c) Maid Marian   d) Rowena

4. What is volcanic flow?
a) mica
b) lava
c) clay
d) flint

5. What is another term for a rocket launch?
a) burnout
b) splashdown
c) reentry
d) blastoff

6. What is a Chinook?
a) wind
b) goat
c) bighorn
d) antelope

7. Which isn't a Romance language?
a) French
b) Swedish
c) Italian
d) Spanish

8. Who was the Greek god of fire?
a) Ares   b) Zeus
c) Apollo   qd) Hephaestus

9. What's another word for plumage?
a) prune jam   b) feathers
c) aged preserves   d) plum pudding

10. Which rope isn't used on an animal?
a) halter   b) leash
c) tether   d) cable

Game #19

1. Who wasn't a knight of the Round Table?
a) Gawain
b) Lancelot
c) Percival
d) Calvin

2. Which word doesn't refer to the countryside?
a) rural
b) urban
c) pastoral
d) bucolic

3. What is the capital of Israel?
a) Jerusalem
b) Tel Aviv
c) Haifa
d) Beersheba

4. In what sport do Pete Sampras and Andre Agassi excel?
a) ice skating
b) baseball
c) tennis
d) basketball

5. What is another word for safari?
a) expedition
b) curry dish
c) safety match
d) street fair

6. Which is not a sailing ship?
a) barkentine
b) sloop
c) schooner
d) cabin cruiser

7. What is a young seal called?
a) fawn
b) calf
c) kitten
d) pup

8. In American history, what was Seward's Folly?

a) Louisiana Purchase

b) Purchase of Alaska

c) 1849 Gold Rush

d) Spanish-American War

9. Which isn't a shaded walk?

a) a breezeway

b) an arcade

c) a boulevard

d) a mall

10. Who is a caretaker of sheep?

a) a tiller

b) a shepherd

c) a plowboy

d) a cowboy

Game #20

1. What is a shillelagh?
a) a love song
b) a club
c) a party
d) an elf

2. What is a stateroom?
a) a ship's cabin
b) a state capitol
c) a parlor
qd) an embassy

3. What is another name for Salisbury steak?
a) T-bone
b) porterhouse
c) filet mignon
d) hamburger

4. What is brine?
a) a form of fuel   b) salt water
c) dirty snow   d) a vegetable

5. What was Samson's vulnerable part?
a) his calf   b) his thumb
c) his hair   d) his thigh

6. Who wasn't a vice-president under Franklin D. Roosevelt?
a) John N. Garner   b) Harry S. Truman
c) Richard M. Nixon   d) Henry Wallace

7. Who is not a city or town official?
a) mayor   b) councilman
c) selectman   d) rector

8. Where is Nob Hill?
a) Boston
b) Montana
c) San Francisco
d) Alabama

9. Who was the Roman god of fire?
a) Mars
b) Vulcan
c) Neptune
d) Morpheus

10. What is a dune?
a) a dumb person
b) an accomplishment
c) a sand hill
d) a brown horse

Game #21

1. Which is an oil well?
a) geyser   b) gusher
c) thermal   d) artesian

2. Men's clothing is often sold in what kind of a store?
a) smithy   b) haberdashery
c) charcuterie   d) greengrocery

3. The Erie Canal is in which state?
a) Vermont   b) Wisconsin
c) Michigan   d) New York

4. What is another word for *siesta*?
a) mountain b) yes
c) nap d) six

5. Which is a woman's voice?
a) tenor b) baritone
c) contralto d) bass

6. What's another term for sitting carelessly?
a) posing b) sprawling
c) perching d) squatting

7. What is a Russian sled?
a) toboggan b) sleigh
c) troika d) travois

8. Which is a fragrant smoke?
a) incense   b) vapor
c) fumes   d) exhaust

9. What is slush?
a) mud   b) lava
c) half-melted snow d) heavy rain

10. Which one's not a soccer player?
a) winger   b) striker
c) tackle   d) goalie

Game #22

1. Which one's not a social gathering?
a) bee
b) tea
c) party
d) boycott

2. Who is the goddess of the earth?
a) Venus
b) Athena
c) Demeter
d) Hera

3. Who is a newly trained soldier?
a) an irregular
b) a recruit
c) a guerrilla
d) a trooper

4. Which is an opera song?
a) lied
b) chant
c) aria
d) ballad

5. What was a serf?
a) a freeman
b) a baron
c) a vassal
d) a knight

6. Which is not a songbird?
a) thrush
b) nightingale
c) lark
d) starling

7. Which one is a space agency?
a) FBI
b) FTC
c) NASA
d) INS

8. Which folk music features castanets?
a) Danish   b) Polish
c) English   d) Spanish

9. *Rio* means river in what language?
a) Russian   b) Burmese
c) Spanish   d) Norwegian

10. Where is the Sphinx located?
a) Bolivia   b) Egypt
c) Guam   d) Bulgaria

Game #23

1. Which is not a water sport?
a) surfing   b) swimming
c) yachting   d) curling

2. What is a moving staircase?
a) a banister   b) an escalator
c) a companionway   d) a tread

3. What is a three-legged stand called?
a) a triangle   b) a triplet
c) a tripod   d) a trifle

4. Which is a shooting star?
a) nova
b) polestar
c) meteor
d) sun

5. What was the home state of Pres. Harry S. Truman?
a) Mississippi
b) Kansas
c) Texas
d) Missouri

6. Which structure is built over water?
a) a tower
b) a bridge
c) a pyramid
d) a steeple

7. Which one isn't a source of sugar?
a) beet
b) cane
c) corn
d) spinach

8. Mary-Kate and Ashley Olsen star in which movie?
a) *It Takes Two*
b) *It's a Wonderful Life*
c) *It's a Mad World*
d) *It Happens Every Spring*

9. What do bears do during the winter?
a) go South
b) shiver
c) hibernate
d) ski

10. Which is not a percussion instrument?
a) cymbal
b) glockenspiel
c) marimba
d) harp

Game #24

1. Where was the birthplace of the Apostle Paul?
a) Jerusalem   b) Jericho
c) Tarsus   d) Rome

2. What is another name for sulfur?
a) phosphorus   b) brimstone
c) quicksilver   d) whitewash

3. Who was Robinson Crusoe's companion?
a) Robin Goodfellow   b) Friday
c) Peter Pan   d) Huck Finn

4. Which is the usual military award?
a) medal   b) token
c) diploma   d) standing applause

5, Which term doesn't mean small talk?
a) gab   b) lecture
c) prattle   d) chat

6. What is the outer covering of teeth called?
a) tartar   b) enamel
c) dentine   d) caries

7. What is a display of temper called?
a) calmness   b) hiccups
c) tantrum   d) humor

8. Which is a ten-year period?
a) decal
b) decibel
c) decimal
d) decade

9. Who are the twins played by Leonardo DiCaprio in *The Man in the Iron Mask*?
a) Cardinals Richelieu and Mazarin
b) Louis XIV and Philippe
c) Aramis and and Athos
d) D'Artagnan and Porthos

10. Where is Mecca?
a) Syria
b) Iran
c) Saudi Arabia
d) Kuwait

Game #25

1. What is another term for scenery?
a) a stage set   b) a prompter's box
c) an actor's role   d) the director's chair

2. What is another term for a campus?
a) military base   b) school grounds
c) a dolphin   d) a house cat

3. Who is not a law officer?
a) bailiff   b) sheriff
c) constable   d) vicar

4. What is the science of animals?
a) agronomy　　　　　b) botany
c) semantics　　　　　d) zoology

5. What is another name for oil cloth?
a) denim　　　　　　b) chiffon
c) linoleum　　　　　d) burlap

6. Who isn't a Scotsman?
a) a Caledonian　　　b) a Highlander
c) a Glaswegian　　　d) a Dubliner

7. What is a Victrola?
a) a phonograph　　　b) a child's stroller
c) a woman's hat　　　d) a man's overcoat

8. Who stars in the movie *Good Burger*?
a) Kenan and Kel   b) Kelly and Kenneth
c) Kathie and Cutie   d) Kerry and Queenie

9. Who wrote the poem "The Raven"?
a) Stephen King   b) John Lennon
c) Edgar Allan Poe   d) Robert Frost

10. Which isn't a policeman's club?
a) nightstick   b) baton
c) billy   d) cudgel

Game #26

1. The Ivy League's Darthmouth College is in which state?
a) Connecticut   b) New Hampshire
c) Massachusetts   d) Maine

2. What is a Pomeranian?
a) a cat   b) a hat
c) an apple   d) a dog

3. What is Popeye's occupation?
a) policeman   b) short-order cook
c) sailor   d) accountant

4. What is a portable lamp called?
a) a lantern   b) a chandelier
c) a sconce   d) a night light

5. What is the seed part or bud of a potato?
a) node   b) tuber
c) eye   d) root

6. Who was the chief Roman god?
a) Jove   b) Vulcan
c) Neptune   d) Morpheus

7. Who makes pottery?
a) carpenter   b) ceramist
c) tinsmith   d) mason

8. What are tapirs, anteaters, and okapis?
a) birds　　　　　b) animals
c) fish　　　　　d) insects

9. What is the season before Easter?
a) Advent　　　　b) Christmas
c) Pentecost　　　d) Lent

10. Which is not an organ of speech?
a) lip　　　　　b) ears
c) tongue　　　　d) throat

Game #27

1. Which is not a veterans' organization?
a) VFW   b) GAR
c) DAV   d) AFL

2. Which city celebrates Bunker Hill Day?
a) New York City   b) Philadelphia
c) Sacramento   d) Boston

3. What is the science of plants?
a) bacteriology   b) ichthyology
c) botany   d) aeronautics

4. What was the pen name of Samuel Clemens?
a) Poor Richard   b) Mark Twain
c) O. Henry   d) Dr. Seuss

5. What's the same as being ill-at-ease?
a) calm   b) collected
c) cool   d) anxious

6. What is the coat of a sheep called?
a) a pelt   b) a fleece
c) a skin   d) a hide

7. Which is a submarine missile?
a) dart   b) arrow
c) bomb   d) torpedo

8. Montevideo is the capital of which South American country?
a) Paraguay
b) Chile
c) Uruguay
d) Argentina

9. What is the shape of a wedge?
a) s-shaped
b) v-shaped
c) l-shaped
d) c-shaped

10. Where would you find a gondola?
a) Venice, Italy
b) Verdun, France
c) Vicennes, Indiana
d) Vail, Colorado

Game #28

1. What's the same as to come into sight?
a) appear
b) disappear
c) vanish
d) depart

2. San Jose is the capital of which country?
a) Costa Rica
b) Honduras
c) Cuba
d) Bolivia

3. In which movie do action figures come to life?
a) *Super Dolls*
b) *Action Packed*
c) *Small Soldiers*
d) *It Figures*

4. What's the opposite of authentic?
a) true   b) fake
c) genuine   d) real

5. Which isn't another term for the North Star?
a) Orion   b) polestar
c) lodestar   d) Polaris

6. Which isn't a place of safety?
a) haven   b) sanctuary
c) refuge   d) thin ice

7. What are iguanas, geckos, and Gila monsters?
a) reptiles   b) birds of prey
c) extra-terrestrials d) amphibians

8. What is a blizzard?
a) rainstorm   b) snowstorm
c) windstorm   d) sandstorm

9. Which is the Empire State?
a) Idaho   b) New York
c) Delaware   d) Rhode Island

10. Which one's not a pack animal?
a) donkey   qb) burro
c) mule   d) zebra

Game #29

1. Which is not a Gospel?
a) James
b) Mark
c) John
d) Matthew

2. What are bullfrogs and salamanders?
a) reptiles
b) amphibians
c) fish
d) birds

3. *Weiss* means white in what language?
a) Russian
b) Cambodian
c) German
d) Finnish

4. Who is associated with Valley Forge, Trenton and Mount Vernon?
a) George Washington b) Herbert Hoover
c) Abraham Lincoln   d) Jerry Ford

5. What does the expression "The walls have ears" mean?
a) holes in the walls   b) secrets can be heard
c) wallpaper has elephants d) Jericho's walls fell
                                       when a trumpet blared

6. Which one is not a noblewoman?
a) countess   b) duchess
c) marchioness   d) seamstress

7. Stowe and Sugarbush are ski resorts in what state?
a) Utah   b) Colorado
c) Vermont   d) California

8. Who was vice-president under John Adams?
a) Thomas Jefferson   b) Aaron Burr
c) DeWitt Clinton   d) John Quincy Adams

9. What's the post of a clergyman in the military?
a) minister   b) chaplain
c) preacher   d) parson

10. Which one doesn't have Dublin as its capital?
a) Hibernia   b) Erin
c) Caledonia   d) Irish Republic

Game #30

1. The Seine flows through which city?
a) Berlin   b) Paris
c) Madrid   d) London

2. Which is a covered passage?
a) aisle   b) arcade
c) walk   d) alley

3. What is a Percheron?
a) giraffe   b) sheep
c) horse   d) dog

4. What are Japanese samurai?
a) craftsmen b) priests
c) warriors d) demons

5. Complete the proverb. "When angry, count to —"
a) one hundred b) you're blue in the face
c) kingdom come d) one hundred thousand

6. Which fruit isn't found in the Bible?
a) fig b) date
c) grape d) banana

7. South Georgia Island in the Atlantic belongs to which country?
a) Spain b) Britain
c) Italy d) Portugal

8. Which one is not usually a covering of cake?
a) frosting   b) icing
c) meringue   d) wafer

9. Where is the Liberty Bell?
a) Philadelphia   b) New York City
c) Boston   d) Washington, DC

10. What building in Arlington, VA has over 23,000 employees?
a) Dept. of Agriculture   b) The Pentagon
c) Library of Congress   d) FBI Headquarters

Game #31

1. Which U.S Service Academy is located in Colorado Springs, CO?
a) Military Academy   b) Naval Academy
c) Coast Guard Academy d) Air Force Academy

2. What is preserving in vinegar called?
a) salting   b) pickling
c) canning   d) smoking

3. Where did Robert E. Lee surrender to Ulysses S. Grant?
a) Manassas   b) Richmond
c) Appomattox   d) Spotsylvania

4. What is played at Wimbledon and Forest Hills?
a) soccer
b) baseball
c) football
d) tennis

5. What is a corsage?
a) a small bouquet
b) a pirate
c) a French island
d) a procession

6. What was the Norse hall of heroes?
a) Olympus
b) Valhalla
c) Midgard
d) Hall of Fame

7. Where are the White Cliffs of Dover?
a) France
b) New Hampshire
c) England
d) Delaware

8. What's another name for the wilde-beest?
a) gnu
b) buffalo
c) musk ox
d) mountain goat

9. What is another term for cotton candy?
a) spun sugar
b) fudge
c) marshmallow
d) candytuft

10. Which is known as the Golden State?
a) Colorado
b) Arizona
c) Nebraska
d) California

Game #32

1. In the Bible, who was the successor to Saul?
a) David
b) Solomon
c) Jonathan
d) Samuel

2. Which isn't a crayfish?
a) a mudbug
b) a crawfish
c) a crawdad
d) a catfish

3. What is a vocation?
a) an occupation
b) a singing voice
c) a holiday
d) a location

4. Where is the Grand Coulee Dam?
a) Oregon   b) Wyoming
c) Washington   d) Montana

5. Brittany, Raul, Victor, and Chris are characters in which soap opera?
a) *General Hospital*   b) *Young and the Restless*
c) *One Life to Live*   d) *Passions*

6. What is another word for sheepwalk?
a) runway   b) road
c) pasture   d) avenue

7. Who was the chief Greek god?
a) Ares   b) Zeus
c) Apollo   d) Hephaestus

8. Which musical instrument doesn't use a reed?
a) saxophone
b) trumpet
c) oboe
d) clarinet

9. Which is not a basketball maneuver?
a) press
b) dribble
c) fast break
d) beanball

10. Which is the largest state here?
a) Wisconsin
b) Utah
c) Maine
d) Kansas

Game #33

1. Sofia is the capital of what country?
a) Bulgaria   b) Belgium
c) Poland   d) Greece

2. Who was the Roman goddess of hunting?
a) Minerva   b) Juno
c) Diana   d) Venus

3. Who was the only Yankee to win the Rookie of the Year Award and MVP?
a) Thurman Munson   b) Mickey Mantle
c) Joe DiMaggio   d) Roger Maris

4. Madeira Island in the Atlantic belongs to what country?
a) Spain
b) Britain
c) Italy
d) Portugal

5. Which isn't a part of a submarine?
a) conning tower
b) mizzenmast
c) torpedo tube
d) periscope

6. Which is not a riddle?
a) conundrum
b) puzzle
c) enigma
d) dimension

7. Where are you most likely to find a curator?
a) on a ranch
b) in a museum
c) in a hospital
d) in a bookstore

8. What is the floor of a ship known as?
a) the deck   b) the galley
c) the mast   d) the keel

9. Rolf, Roman, and Chloe are characters
in which soap opera?
a) *As the World Turns*   b) *All My Children*
c) *Bold and the Beautiful* d) *Days of Our Lives*

10. What was the nickname of President
Dwight D. Eisenhower?
a) Doug   b) Black Jack
c) Ike   d) Stonewall

Game #34

1. What is another name for the disease polio?
a) typhus
b) infantile paralysis
c) smallpox
d) cholera

2. Who are the two nasty aunts in the movie *James and the Giant Peach*?
a) Spitball and Snail
b) Spiker and Sponge
c) Sneaky and Snake
d) Snarl and Squeal

3. What is a ship's company?
a) the crew
b) a corporation
c) invited guests
d) the rest of the fleet

4. Which one was a Roman emperor?
a) Nero
b) Zero
c) Hero
d) Gyro

5. In the movie *A Little Princess*, who plays Sara Crewe?
a) Eleanor Bron
b) Liesel Matthews
c) Vanessa Lee Chester
d) Elizabeth Chandler

6. Who was the only major leaguer to serve in both World Wars?
a) Grover Cleveland Alexander
b) Ted Williams
c) Hank Gowdy
d) Casey Stengel

7. Which isn't a wall painting?
a) mural
b) fresco
c) tapestry
d) panel

8. Name the Shannen Doherty character in *Beverly Hills 90201*.

a) Barbara b) Brenda
c) Brittany d) Babs

9. Who starred in the teen soap opera *Swan's Crossing*?

a) Sarah Michelle Gellar b) Sarah Jessica Parker
c) Molly Stanton d) Kristina Sisca

10. What was the pen name of Benjamin Franklin?

a) Poor Richard b) Mark Twain
c) O. Henry d) Dr. Seuss

Game #35

1. What is the theme song of the TV show *Cops*?
a) "Jailhouse Rock"   b) "Bad Boys"
c) "A Policeman's Lot"   d) "Stop in the Name of Love!"

2. What is a Scottish accent?
a) a brogue   b) a drawl
c) a burr   d) a twang

3. The Eiffel Tower is in what European capital?
a) Brussels   b) Madrid
c) Copenhagen   d) Paris

4. Who is the emcee on *The Price is Right*?
a) Growler
b) Barker
c) Leno
d) Letterman

5. Which plant is not painful to touch?
a) briar
b) nettle
c) gardenia
d) thistle

6. What is a windbreaker?
a) a jacket
b) hurricane fencing
c) a gauge
d) a bonanza

7. Who won the most consecutive batting awards— a record nine?
a) Rod Carew
b) Honus Wagner
c) Ty Cobb
d) Rogers Hornsby

8. Who played TV's Dr. Heathcliff Huxstable?
a) Dick Van Dyke   b) Tom Bosley
c) Bill Cosby   d) Alan Alda

9. What is a company of performers called?
a) team   b) squad
c) troupe   d) crew

10. Which one is not a period or part of a game?
a) inning   b) frame
c) quarter   d) fifth

Game #36

1. Which isn't a book of the Hebrew Bible?
a) Hebrews
b) Ezra
c) Job
d) Isaiah

2. Who does Christina Ricci play in the movie *Gold Diggers: Secret of Bear Mountain*?
a) Babe
b) Betty-Ann
c) Beth
d) Eliza

3. Where are Atlantic City and Princeton University?
a) New York
b) New Jersey
c) Nebraska
d) Nevada

4. Which language was spoken in ancient Rome?
a) Latin   b) Russian
c) Chinese   d) Korean

5. Which pitcher here has thrown a perfect game?
a) Sandy Koufax   b) Allie Reynolds
c) Nolan Ryan   d) Whitey Ford

6. What is a hot line?
a) an overheated cable   b) an emergency phone
c) a steam pipe   d) an exhaust pipe

7. Where is Rice University?
a) Hong Kong   b) Houston
c) Honduras   d) Honshu

8. Who invented dynamite?
a) Eli Whitney   b) James Watt
c) Alfred Nobel   d) Samuel Colt

9. What is the Iron City?
a) Toledo   b) Gary
c) Pittsburgh   d) Detroit

10. Which character does not appear in *Ivanhoe*?
a) Rowena   b) Rebecca
c) Friar Tuck   d) King Arthur

Game #37

1. Who was the first baseball player to receive $100,000 for a single season?
a) Joe DiMaggio   b) Babe Ruth
c) Mickey Mantle   d) Jackie Robinson

2. What is another word for silver-tongued?
a) precious   b) eloquent
c) gold-toothed   d) wealthy

3. Who is not a Bible prophet?
a) Amos   b) Saul
c) Daniel   d) Elijah

4. What is a female kangaroo called?
a) doe   b) mare
c) vixen   d) cow

5. Which country is not on the Mediterranean?
a) Greece   b) France
c) Belgium   d) Italy

6. Which state celebrates Kamehameha Day?
a) Wisconsin   b) Oregon
c) Nebraska   d) Hawaii

7. Which is a mixture of metals?
a) solder   b) ingot
c) alloy   d) foil

8. Who is credited with inventing radio?
a) Isaac Newton   b) Guglielmo Marconi
c) Louis Pasteur   d) William Harvey

9. Cairo is the capital of what country?
a) Morocco   b) Syria
c) Egypt   d) Tunisia

10. What is a "John Hancock"?
a) a signature   b) a shoe style
c) a type of dessert   d) a horse race

Game #38

1. Which is the Wolverine State?
a) Minnesota   b) Wisconsin
c) North Dakota   d) Michigan

2. What is a mimeograph?
a) a duplicator   b) an impersonator
c) a signature   d) a movie projector

3. What is a lodestone?
a) a magnetic mineral   b) a heavy rock
c) ballast   d) a treasure trove

4. What is a troubadour?
a) a horseman
b) a singer
c) a physician
d) a farmer

5. What is a monocle?
a) a lizard
b) a marmoset
c) an eyeglass
d) a mutt

6. What is another way of saying skin-deep?
a) cheap
b) shallow
c) fraudulent
d) tattooed

7. What does the Montana state motto "Oro y Plata" mean?
a) "Take any dish"
b) "Gold and Silver"
c) "The mine is on a plateau"
d) "Our plates are golden"

8. Where was Napoleon born?
a) Corsica
b) Malta
c) Sicily
d) Sardinia

9. What is the science of the nervous system?
a) neurology
b) podiatry
c) dentistry
d) dermatology

10. New Brunswick is a province of what country?
a) Great Britain
b) Australia
c) Canada
d) New Zealand

Game #39

1. Who was the Wizard of Menlo Park?
a) Albert Einstein   b) Lou Gehrig
c) Jonas Salk   d) Thomas Alva Edison

2. Who said it and where: "It doesn't make any sense. That's why I trust it."?
a) Kate Winslet   b) Leonardo DiCaprio
   in *Titanic*   in *The Beach*
c) Drew Barrymore   d) Jodi Lyn O'Keefe
   in *Never Been Kissed*   in *She's All That*

3. What is Camp David?
a) a religious center   b) a presidential hideaway
c) an Army camp   d) a Boy Scout camp

4. Who was the Sun King?
a) Louis XIV
b) Napoleon Bonaparte
c) George III
d) Kaiser Wilhelm

5. Delores Hall stars on what TV show?
a) *Diagnosis Murder*
b) *Ally McBeal*
c) *JAG*
d) *The Nanny*

6. What is an inventor's right to his invention?
a) trademark
b) patent
c) copyright
d) registration

7. Who was the Little Corporal?
a) Adolf Hitler
b) Napoleon Bonaparte
c) Richard III
d) Julius Caesar

8. Lagos is the capital of which African country?
a) Tunisia b) Nigeria
c) Libya d) Ethiopia

9. What's the prize cup in tennis?
a) Davis b) Heisman
c) Stanley d) America's

10. What do baseball fans do in the seventh inning?
a) stretch b) leave
c) talk with the players d) argue with the umpire

Game #40

1. What is Norway's government?
a) republic
b) limited monarchy
c) federation
d) confederation

2. What best defines an optimist?
a) watchful
b) far-sighted
c) upbeat
d) learned

3. What's another term for a noun?
a) adjective
b) adverb
c) substantive
d) modifier

4. Which state capital is named for a German politician?
a) St. Paul, MN   b) Albany, NY
c) Bismarck, ND   d) Trenton, NJ

5. What is any number under ten called?
a) cardinal   b) digit
c) prime   d) integer

6. What's another word for blacksmith?
a) farrier   b) carpenter
c) mason   d) plumber

7. In which movie is Adam Sandler a spoiled heir who has to repeat school?
a) *Richie Rich*   b) *Billy Madison*
c) *Arthur*   d) *Trading Places*

8. What is another word for inkling?
a) ink blot
b) small pen
c) hint
d) autograph

9. How are the children of Mary and her sister Jane related?
a) second cousins
b) first cousins
c) first cousins once removed
d) second cousins twice removed

10. What is a diagram in mathematics?
a) a map
b) a picture
c) a graph
d) a view

Game #41

1. What is a corral?
a) a livestock enclosure   b) a dish from India
c) lobster eggs   d) a pinkish color

2. What does a milliner do?
a) sew dresses   b) grind grain
c) sell newspapers   d) make hats

3. Among the Norse gods, who was Loki?
a) god of mischief   b) god of war
c) god of crops   d) god of the ocean

4. Which instrument helps a musician keep time?
a) pitch pipe
b) mandolin
c) dulcimer
d) metronome

5. Which is not a North African country?
a) Tunisia
b) Algeria
c) Morocco
d) Eritrea

6. Which is the Old Dominion State?
a) South Carolina
b) Maryland
c) Virginia
d) Florida

7. Pitchblende is the ore of what mineral?
a) platinum
b) tin
c) uranium
d) mercury

8. What are orthographers concerned with?

a) spelling   b) maps
c) politics   d) medicine

9. Which opera did Verdi not write?

a) *Il Trovatore*   b) *La Traviata*
c) *Carmen*   d) *Aida*

10. What is the term for free postage privilege that certain government executives enjoy?

a) franking   b) postage-free
c) postpaid   d) business reply mail

Game #42

1. In what movie does Michael Jordan fight aliens?
a) *Space Jam*   b) *Space Children*
c) *Spaceballs*   d) *Spaced Out*

2. Where was the Ottoman Empire?
a) Peru   b) Turkey
c) Germany   d) Japan

3. To run amok means to be out of what?
a) school   b) time
c) control   d) money

4. Which word has nothing to do with the outback?
a) bush
b) wilderness
c) suburbs
d) backwoods

5. Which language isn't commonly spoken in Pakistan?
a) Gaelic
b) Punjabi
c) Urdu
d) Baluchi

6. What is the jail of a ship called?
a) the galley
b) the mast
c) the brig
d) the keel

7. Where is the palate located?
a) nose
b) ear
c) palm
d) mouth

8. What is the Big Ditch?
a) Grand Canyon
b) Death Valley
c) Panama Canal
d) Sun Valley

9. What is the Ringed Planet?
a) Saturn
b) Jupiter
c) Mars
d) Pluto

10. What famous battlefield is in Pennsylvania?
a) Little Big Horn
b) Gettysburg
c) The Alamo
d) Bull Run

Game #43

1. Who was the only pitcher to hit three home runs in a game?
a) Cy Young
b) Don Newcombe
c) Jim Tobin
d) Warren Spahn

2. What is a shepherd's staff called?
a) a crook
b) a brook
c) a crock
d) a sock

3. Simon Bolivar was the liberator of what country?
a) Portugal
b) Poland
c) Peru
d) Pakistan

4. Who aren't Plains Indians?
a) Ute   b) Pawnee
c) Sioux   d) Seminole

5. Which is the brightest planet?
a) Mercury   b) Uranus
c) Mars   d) Venus

6. Which is the Pelican State?
a) Alabama   b) Texas
c) Louisiana   d) Florida

7. What is another name for a switchboard?
a) control panel   b) fuse box
c) dashboard   d) gear cluster

8. What does ritzy mean?
a) fashionable   b) tacky
c) dated   d) shabby

9. Which one is not the arm of a river?
a) fork   b) estuary
c) bed   d) tributary

10. Who starred as Maggie Carpenter in
The Runaway Bride?
a) Goldie Hawn   b) Drew Barrymore
c) Julia Roberts   d) Sandra Bullock

Game #44

1. What is the sacred river of India?
a) Rhine   b) Ganges
c) Nile   d) Lethe

2. What was the name of President Franklin D. Roosevelt's wife?
a) Sara   b) Betsy
c) Eleanor   d) Martha

3. Who was a foe of the Crusaders?
a) Genghis Khan   b) Saladin
c) Montezuma   d) Attila the Hun

4. What is the periodic motion of the sea called?
a) swell
b) surf
c) waves
d) tide

5. What is a fortnight?
a) a moonless night
b) two weeks
c) overtime
d) an unlit fortress

6. What is a shaddock?
a) a fish
b) a fruit
c) a dry dock
d) a lampshade

7. Who was Sitting Bull's enemy?
a) Tecumseh
b) Cochise
c) Geronimo
d) Custer

8. Which one's not a Slav?
a) Serb   b) Bulgarian
c) Czech   d) Albanian

9. What is South Carolina's capital?
a) Columbia   b) Spartanburg
c) Charleston   d) Rock Hill

10. Which of these has nothing to do with Superman?
a) Lois Lane   b) Daily Planet
c) Clark Kent   d) Shazam

Game #45

1. What's the first name of ___ Wachs on TV's *Profiler*?
a) Kathleen   b) Caitlin
c) Catherine   d) Kathy

2. Where would you most likely find a fjord?
a) Hawaii   b) Norway
c) Cambodia   d) Hungary

3. Where is Fort Sumter located?
a) Maryland   b) Texas
c) South Carolina   d) Florida

4. Where does a baseball pitcher warm up?
a) bullpen   b) mound
c) dugout   d) infield

5. Who isn't a South Sea islander?
a) Maori   b) Inuit
c) Polynesian   d) Samoan

6. Which one is not a string instrument?
a) violin   b) guitar
c) celeste   d) lyre

7. What is a young swan called?
a) pen   b) cygnet
c) cob   d) swanny

8. Which country is William Tell associated with?
a) France
b) Italy
c) Switzerland
d) Germany

9. What did Triceratops dinosaurs carry around on their heads?
a) three horns
b) a helmet
c) another eye
d) a baseball cap

10. Who was Tarzan's mate?
a) Jane
b) Joan
c) June
d) Jean

Game #46

1. Bianca (Larisa Oleynik) can't date until her sister (Julia Stiles) finds a boyfriend. Name the movie.

a) *10 Things I Hate About You*

b) *The Taming of the Shrew*

c) *Kiss Me Kate*

d) *Shakespeare in Love*

2. Where are the Black Hills?

a) Montana

b) South Dakota

c) Nebraska

d) Vermont

3. Where is Canterbury?

a) Scotland

b) England

c) Wales

d) Ireland

4. How many players are there usually on a polo team?
a) seven   b) six
c) four   d) five

5. What is a count of people called?
a) an accounting   b) a census
c) a vote   d) a referendum

6. What is porcelain?
a) a fruit   b) chinaware
c) a pig   d) a hedgehog

7. To whom did Timor, Angola and Mozambique once belong?
a) Spain   b) France
c) Italy   d) Portugal

8. Which of the following is pictured on the dollar bill?

a) an obelisk

b) the Coliseum

c) a pyramid

d) the Great Wall of China

9. With what country is Sanskrit associated?

a) Iraq

b) India

c) Iran

d) Italy

10. What is a prawn?

a) a chess piece

b) collateral for a loan

c) a shrimp

d) a boat

Game #47

1. Which Boston Celtic was never named
NBA MVP?
a) Larry Bird   b) Bob Cousy
c) Kevin McHale   d) Bill Russell

2. *Ami* means friend in what language?
a) Thai   b) Polish
c) French   d) Norwegian

3. Who is not a member of a ship's crew?
a) hand   b) mate
c) purser   d) accountant

4. What day of the week is named for the chief Norse god?
a) Tuesday
b) Wednesday
c) Thursday
qd) Friday

5. Which country sold us Alaska?
a) France
b) Denmark
c) Canada
d) Russia

6 Which country celebrates Dominion Day?
a) United States
b) Canada
c) Mexico
d) Great Britain

7. Who was president just before Franklin D. Roosevelt?
a) Calvin Coolidge
b) Theodore Roosevelt
c) Herbert Hoover
d) Harry S. Truman

8. What is the symbol of Princeton University?
a) chipmunk
b) goat
c) tiger
d) donkey

9. Which dinosaurs stole the eggs of other dinosaurs?
a) Ovines
b) Oviraptors
c) Eggcentricsaur
d) Foxosaur and Weaselosaur

10. Who isn't a queen in the Bible?
a) Candace
b) Sheba
c) Esther
c) Deborah

Game #48

1. Edmonton is the capital of which Canadian province?
a) Alberta
b) British Columbia
c) Manitoba
d) Newfoundland

2. What is another name for the American Staffordshire terrier?
a) pit bull
b) Boston terrier
c) El Toro
d) mastiff

3. Which isn't a Colorado park?
a) Rocky Mountain
b) Estes
c) Yosemite
d) Mesa Verde

4. What is the edge of a road called?
a) bend   b) hairpin
c) shoulder   d) leg

5. Who settled the Southwest after the Native Americans?
a) French missionaries   b) Texan cowboys
c) gold rush prospectors d) Spaniards and Mexicans

6. What is Earth's path around the sun called?
a) revolution   b) orbit
c) rotation   d) compass

7. Who conquered the Aztecs?
a) Ferdinand Magellan b) Vasco da Gama
c) Hernando Cortes   d) Francisco Pizarro

8. What is the capital of Connecticut?
a) Westport   b) New Haven
c) Hartford   d) Stamford

9. Which isn't a constellation?
a) Taurus   b) Pisces
c) Ursa Major   d) Venus

10. Which is the legendary "lost" continent?
a) Eurasia   b) Atlantis
c) Cascadia   d) Antarctica

Game #49

1. What is the office machine that destroys unwanted papers?
a) a chopper
b) a shredder
c) a grinder
d) an atomizer

2. What is the capital of Ecuador?
a) Quito
b) San Juan
c) Lima
d) Bogota

3. What is the largest breed of terrier?
a) Airedale
b) Cairn
c) Lakeland
d) Sealyham

4. What is a dreadnought?
a) a battleship
b) a brave person
c) a dragon
d) a zero on a test

5. Which island is not near Europe?
a) Elba
b) Crete
c) Mindanao
d) Corsica

6. In the movie *The Fifth Element*, what character does Bruce Willis play?
a) a cab driver
b) a nuclear scientist
c) a lobster fisherman
d) an art teacher

7. What mythological creature had snakes for hair?
a) The Sphinx
b) Medusa
c) Circe
d) Loki

8. Which dinosaur's eggs and nest were discovered first?

a) Adasaurus

b) Edmontosaurus

c) Protoceratops

d) Acrocanthosaurus

9. What was the Studebaker?

a) a sea monster

b) an automobile

c) an oven

d) a type of chef

10. Name the first woman U.S. Supreme Court Justice.

a) Sandra Day O'Connor

b) Ruth Bader Ginsberg

c) Marcia Clark

d) Judge Judy

Game #50

1. Which one is not an expert in jewels?
a) lapidary   b) appraiser
c) gemologist   d) coroner

2. In the Bible, who was the wife of Ahab?
a) Salome   b) Bathsheba
c) Jezebel   d) Lilith

3. What is the same as joining the colors?
a) marrying   b) enlisting
c) waving the flag   d) merging companies

4. Which isn't a joint?
a) hip   b) knee
c) femur   d) wrist

5. What is slang for an apprentice reporter?
a) fawn   b) pup
c) cub   d) colt

6. Who is the puppet Judy's husband?
a) Punch   b) Joe
c) Jack   d) Romeo

7. What is June 14th?
a) Arbor Day   b) Flag Day
c) Midsummer's Day   d) Commencement Day

8. What sound is heard in a kennel?
a) neigh b) chirp
c) cluck d) bark

9. Who said, "Ask not what your country can do for you; ask what you can do for your country?"
a) Robert Kennedy b) Edward Kennedy
c) John F. Kennedy d) Teddy Roosevelt

10. What is the history of a person's life called?
a) diary b) file
c) biography d) classified info

Game #51

1. What was the mythological horse with a horn?
a) hippo
b) rhino
c) walrus
d) unicorn

2. Which vegetable is called "iceberg"?
a) carrot
b) parsnip
c) lettuce
d) beet

3. What are a soldier's dog tags?
a) dog license
b) driver's license
c) personal identification
d) his medals

4. Santa Claus Land is found in what state?
a) Alaska
b) Minnesota
c) North Dakota
d) Indiana

5. Which is not a leaping insect?
a) grasshopper
b) locust
c) cricket
d) termite

6. The Mississippi River town of Davenport is in what state?
a) Iowa
b) Minnesota
c) Missouri
d) Louisiana

7. In which country is Persian the major language?
a) Russia
b) Iran
c) Tunisia
d) Honduras

8. The shamrock is the emblem of which country?
a) France
b) Cuba
c) Ireland
d) Laos

9. Which island is famous for its giant lizards?
a) Easter
b) Komodo
c) New Guinea
d) Capri

10. According to the proverb, what doesn't pay?
a) crime
b) free admission
c) a senior citizen
d) crying

Game #52

1. How many men are in a chess set?
a) twenty-five
b) twenty
c) thirty
d) thirty-two

2. Who were Currier & Ives?
a) dancers
b) movie actors
c) print-makers
d) explorers

3. In the nursery rhyme, what was Jack Horner's prize?
a) a marble
b) a plum
c) a gold coin
d) a sword

Game #55

1. What is a fen?
a) a native of Finland
b) a sports enthusiast
c) a marshy region
d) part of a fish

2. Which island was leased by Britain from China in 1898 for 99 years?
a) Singapore
b) Hong Kong
c) Formosa
d) Bali

3. What city is known as Gotham?
a) Boston
b) Washington, DC
c) New York City
d) London

4. What is an Irish accent called?
a) a burr
b) a stammer
c) a twang
d) a brogue

5. Where is Dulles International Airport?
a) San Francisco, CA
b) Washington, DC
c) Dubuque, IA
d) Memphis, TN

6. Who ceded Guam to the U.S. in 1898?
a) France
b) Japan
c) Spain
d) China

7. What is Fontainebleau?
a) a mineral spring
b) a French palace and forest
c) a shade of blue
d) Kentucky's capital

8. In mythology, who cleaned the Augean Stables?
a) Perseus   b) Theseus
c) Hercules   d) Hector

9. Which event happened at Kitty Hawk, NC for the first time?
a) airplane flight   b) radio message
c) moon rocket   d) TV show

10. Which country was once known as Cathay?
a) Japan   b) Thailand
c) Vietnam   d) China

Game #5

1. Who cut the Gordian Knot?
a) Darius   b) Mark Anthony
c) Alexander the Great d) Nero

2. U.S. Navy Lt. Pinkerton appears in which opera?
a) *The Mikado*   b) *Aida*
c) *Carmen*   d) *Madame Butterfly*

3. In which sport do you find a gutter and alley?
a) curling   b) field hockey
c) bowling   d) cricket

4. What is a yellow jacket?

a) a mammal   b) an insect

c) a golfer's garment   d) a coward

5. Where did the Los Angeles Dodgers originally come from?

a) Tucson   b) Houston

c) Brooklyn   d) Philadelphia

6. Where are the Hebrides Islands?

a) Greenland   b) Scotland

c) New Zealand   d) Maine

7. What is a Donnybrook?

a) Marie Osmond's brother   b) a creek

c) a riot   d) a Spanish man

8. The name of which state capital was formerly Last Chance Gulch?
a) Helena, MT
b) St. Paul, MN
c) Austin, TX
d) Sacramento, CA

9. What was the Golden Horde?
a) a South American mine
b) Russian conquerors
c) a Turkish inlet
d) a Californian bridge

10. What was the former name of the Hawaiian Islands?
a) the Marianas
b) Midway
c) the Sandwich Islands
d) the Solomon Islands

4. Which game is similar to jai-alai?
a) basketball   b) soccer
c) hockey   d) handball

5. Sayonara is good-bye in what language?
a) Chinese   b) Korean
c) Japanese   d) Hawaiian

6. Who was Dr. Jekyll's other personality?
a) Dr. Fell   b) Mr. Hyde
c) Bluebeard   d) Sam Hall

7. *Little House on the Prairie* is set in what state?
a) Iowa   b) Illinois
b) Missouri   d) Kansas

8. Katmandu is the capital of what country?
a) Tibet
b) Iran
c) Nepal
d) India

9. What is another name for kettle-drums?
a) cymbals
b) bass drums
c) timpani
d) drum set

10. Who was Captain Kidd?
a) an explorer
b) a pirate
c) a cavalry leader
d) a conqueror

Game #53

1. In what book is Toad Hall found?
a) *Kim*   b) *Huckleberry Finn*
c) *The Wind*   d) *Alice in*
   in the Willows   *Wonderland*

2. On what food and drink did the Greek gods live?
a) manna   b) tacos
c) nectar and ambrosia   d) pizza pie

3. Who was the Roman equivalent of the Greek goddess Aphrodite?
a) Minerva   b) Juno
c) Diana   d) Venus

4. What did Roy Chapman Andrews discover in the Gobi Desert?
a) fossil dinosaur eggs　　b) first horse
c) mammoth elephant　　d) Mt. Olympus

5. What legendary group did Jason lead?
a) The Argonauts　　b) The Trojans
c) The Gods　　d) The Giants

6. Which Baltic country was not part of the Soviet Union?
a) Finland　　b) Estonia
c) Latvia　　d) Lithuania

7. Benedict Arnold's treachery happened during which war?
a) Civil War　　b) French & Indian War
c) Revolutionary War　　d) Spanish-American War

8. Gurkha soldiers come from which country?
a) India
b) Pakistan
c) Nepal
d) Bangladesh

9. In what kind of auction is the price lowered, not raised?
a) contrary auction
b) upside-down auction
c) Dutch auction
d) mixed-up auction

10. Where did the Habsburgs rule?
a) Norway
b) Austria-Hungary
c) Russia
d) France

Game #56

1. What does the army phrase "going AWOL" mean?
a) being absent without leave
b) reporting to a warrant officer
c) watching for a lieutenant
d) working after hours

2. Where in South America is Ecuador located?
a) Pacific coast
b) Atlantic coast
c) center
d) southernmost tip

3. Where is the Garden of the Gods?
a) India
b) near the Amazon
c) Colorado Springs
d) Siberia

4. Where is the Hague?
a) Switzerland   b) The Netherlands
c) Belgium   d) Denmark

5. Whose birthright did Jacob buy?
a) Joseph's   b) David's
c) Esau's   d) Joshua's

6. What is the top harness horse race?
a) Hambletonian   b) Belmont
c) Preakness   d) Kentucky Derby

7. Who ruled Haiti before it got its independence?
a) Spain   b) England
c) France   d) United States

8. To what town did the Pied Piper come to clear out the rats?
a) Hamburg
b) Hamelin
c) Hampshire
d) Hampton

9. Where is Harpers Ferry, the arsenal John Brown tried to seize?
a) South Carolina
b) Virginia
c) Georgia
d) West Virginia

10. What is another word for France?
a) Franklin
b) Franconia
c) Gaul
d) Francois

Game #57

1. Gen. Sherman's 1864 campaign is recalled by what song?
a) "Dixie"
b) "Way Down Upon the Swanee River"
c) "Marching Through Georgia"
d) "My Old Kentucky Home"

2. What was the name of the immigrant station in New York harbor?
a) Ellis Island
b) Bedloe's Island
c) Welfare Island
d) Roosevelt Island

3. What language is spoken in Austria?
a) Austrian
b) Swiss
c) German
d) Viennese

4. In what country is Esperanto the mother tongue?
a) China
b) Paraguay
c) Okinawa
d) no place

5. Who rules Gibraltar?
a) Spain
b) Britain
c) Morocco
d) France

6. What is Eton?
a) a British boys school
b) a Welsh racetrack
c) a Dutch band
d) a restaurant chain

7. Where was actor Sean Connery born?
a) Glasgow, Scotland
b) Liverpool, England
c) Dublin, Ireland
d) Sydney, Australia

8. Who was Fargo, ND named after?

a) No one. It meant Fargo was far to go.

b) W. G. Fargo of Wells Fargo

c) Capt. Frank Fargo

d) Fargo Dust Company

9. Which Portuguese territory was annexed by India in 1961?

a) Sri Lanka

b) Seychelles Islands

c) Goa

d) Benares

10. What is a temporary platform?

a) boardwalk

b) scaffold

c) deck

d) stand

Game #58

1. Cinnabar is the ore of which mineral?
a) platinum   b) tin
c) uranium   d) mercury

2. Which state celebrates Seward's Day?
a) Hawaii   b) Mississippi
c) Alaska   d) Delaware

3. Charon ferried dead souls across what river?
a) Styx   b) Amazon
c) Nile   d) Ganges

4. What was the name of the mountain where the Greek gods lived?
a) Valhalla
b) Olympus
c) Vesuvius
d) Everest

5. What was George Washington's occupation as a young man?
a) river boat captain
b) surveyor
c) electrician
d) messenger boy

6. Which dog isn't a spaniel?
a) Clumber
b) Cocker
c) Norfolk
d) Skye

7. Which is the Hawkeye State?
a) Indiana
b) Illinois
c) Iowa
d) Idaho

8. The Civil War took place during which time period?
a) 1776-1800   b) 1820-1850
c) 1850-1870   d) 1870-1900

9. Which isn't a poultry breed?
a) Staffordshire   b) Leghorn
c) Rhode Island Red   d) Plymouth Rock

10. Which is not a young plant?
a) seedling   b) shoot
c) sprout   d) stump

Game #59

1. What kind of animal is a cow?
a) equine　　　　　　b) feline
c) canine　　　　　　d) bovine

2. Where is the northernmost point of the United States?
a) Duluth, MN　　　　　b) Point Barrow, AK
c) West Quoddy Head, ME　d) Seattle, WA

3. What is a mud puppy?
a) a dirty young dog　　b) an amphibian
c) a fish　　　　　　　d) a bird

4. Which university isn't in Georgia?
a) Emory
b) Oglethorpe
c) Mercer
d) Vanderbilt

5. What is the Green Mountain State?
a) Virginia
b) Alaska
c) Vermont
d) Montana

6. What was Linus Pauling's great achievement?
a) five unsuccessful runs for President
b) he won two Nobel Prizes
c) he invented cereal
d) oldest man to win Olympic gold

7. Which one isn't a Powerpuff Girl?
a) Blossom
b) Buffy
c) Bubbles
d) Buttercup

8. Which is not a Channel Island?
a) Wight
b) Sark
c) Jersey
d) Guernsey

9. Which is the Gopher State?
a) Wisconsin
b) Maine
c) Arkansas
d) Minnesota

10. Which country celebrates Holi?
a) Denmark
b) India
c) Paraguay
d) Japan

Game #60

1. What does a polo player hit the ball with?
a) racket   b) mallet
c) bat   d) paddle

2. John D. Rockefeller made his millions in what commodity?
a) oil   b) ice
c) wool   d) corn

3. Which is the largest planet here?
a) Venus   b) Jupiter
c) Saturn   d) Mars

4. In which sport do you find stones and brooms?
a) curling
b) field hockey
c) bowling
d) cricket

5. Which National Park features natural thermal waters?
a) Isle Royale, MI
b) Hot Springs, AR
c) Kings Canyon, CA
d) Mt. Rainier, WA

6. Jamal and Chris are characters in which soap opera?
a) *Port Charles*
b) *Guiding Light*
c) *One Life to Live*
d) *Passions*

7. What is aspirin's technical name?
a) sulfuric acid
b) citric acid
c) acetylsalicylic acid
d) muriatic acid

8. In the Charge of the Light Brigade, what country did the charging?
a) Russia
b) Turkey
c) Germany
d) Great Britain

9. Rhodesian Ridgeback dogs are used to hunt what animals?
a) raccoons
b) lions
c) rabbits
d) badgers

10. Who invented the lightning rod?
a) Samuel Graham Bell
b) Eli Whitney
c) Benjamin Franklin
d) Louis Pasteur

ANSWERS

Game #1
1. d) hen 2. a) Genesis 3. c) an egg 4. c) harpoon 5. d) dew
6. b) heehaw 7. c) sheep 8. a) forfeit 9. b) a goat or a nursemaid
10. c) imaginary

Game #2
1. c) Christmas 2. b) subtract 3. c) acorn 4. c) ewe 5. d) hoot
6. d) anxious 7. c) cone 8. c) lane 9. b) Lightning 10. c) appear

Game #3.
1. d) hiss 2. c) Moscow 3. a) swab 4. a) assist 5. c) Estonia
6. a) forest 7. c) stapler 8. a) xylophone 9. d) hopscotch
10. c) spurious

Game #4
1. b) third rail 2. c) fuselage 3. d) tabloid 4. b) Windsor knot
5. b) turtleneck 6. c) hefty 7. d) scythe 8. d) ton 9. c) first light
10. c) Georgia

Game #5
1. b) a sheepdog 2. b) a diploma 3. b) humming
4. c) shoes & snakes 5. c) play 6. d) Hawaii 7. d) New Orleans
8. a) cymbal 9. d) a launch pad 10. a) pip

Game #6
1. c) a muggle 2. b) Louisa May Alcott 3. d) inning
4. a) Tommy Lee Jones 5. c) dog 6. a) Kristen Johnston
7. b) a hot dog 8. b) Picard 9. c) clarinet 10. a) news anchor

Game #7

1. b) an explosive 2. c) screwdriver 3. c) caboose 4. c) oak
5. b) subway 6. d) giddyap 7. c) stand-in 8. c) Nippon 9. b) karma
10. c) reptiles

Game #8

1. d) Thor 2. d) sixty 3. b) an insect 4. b) cache 5. a) insult
6. a) never 7. d) pomegranate 8. c) Mississippi 9. d) haggis
10. c) Annapolis

Game #9

1. a) Venus 2. c) Sun Valley 3. b) Illinois 4. d) unlawful
5. d) goulash 6. d) cider 7. c) Romeo 8. b) Topeka
9. c) *The Mikado* 10. b) kind

Game #10

1. d) helmsman 2. b) el toro 3. c) rhetoric 4. c) Mayflower
5. c) veteran 6. d) Massachusetts 7. d) Solomon 8. c) serape
9. a) midday 10. c) Special Forces

Game #11

1. b) a tower 2. c) asbestos 3. b) graphite 4. d) St. Paul
5. c) Miriam 6. a) Kansas 7. c) quartet 8. c) cotton
9. c) encampment 10. d) Missouri

Game #12

1. a) a white whale 2. d) a type of coffee 3. a) a tooth
4. d) Monaco 5. c) a graduate's hat 6. b) praying mantis
7. c) trombone 8. d) Italy 9. a) old horse 10. c) nee

Game #13

1. c) Italy 2. a) a knot 3. c) a flyer 4. c) corporal
5. c) Long John Silver 6. a) jeepers creepers 7. d) dickie
8. b) an eye 9. b) riveting 10. c) Nepal

Game #14

1. d) *Passions* 2. a) the sea 3. d) Edinburgh 4. c) spatula
5. c) mountain man 6. b) aerie 7. c) flipper 8. b) nickelodeon
9. a) Ararat 10. c) serf

Game #15

1. a) Mars 2. c) snow and rain 3. c) adjutant 4. b) oil prospector
5. c) tithing 6. b) marsupials 7. d) Persian 8. a) frontier
9. c) wildebeest 10. c) palette

Game #16

1. b) Islamabad 2. c) panda 3. c) Italian 4. d) chaps
5. c) Samson 6. b) a stub 7. d) Paris 8. b) debut
9. a) octogenarian 10. a) charitable

Game #17

1. d) a rookery 2. d) indigent 3. a) mat 4. c) one thousand
5. c) chief petty officer 6. a) catamaran 7. c) a pirate flag
8. a) left-handed person 9. c) star-spangled 10. c) Mars

Game #18

1. d) howl 2. d) a tree 3. c) Maid Marian 4. b) lava 5. d) blastoff
6. a) wind 7. b) Swedish 8. d) Hephaestus 9. b) feathers
10. d) cable

Game #19
1. d) Calvin 2. b) urban 3. a) Jerusalem 4. c) tennis
5. a) expedition 6. d) cabin cruiser 7. d) pup
8. b) Purchase of Alaska 9. c) a boulevard 10. b) a shepherd

Game #20
1. b) a club 2. a) a ship's cabin 3. d) hamburger 4. b) salt water
5. c) his hair 6. c) Richard M. Nixon 7. d) rector
8. c) San Francisco 9. b) Vulcan 10. c) a sand hill

Game #21
1. b) gusher 2. b) haberdashery 3. d) New York
4. c) nap 5. c) contralto 6. b) sprawling 7. c) troika 8. a) incense
9. c) half-melted snow 10. c) tackle

Game #22
1. d) boycott 2. c) Demeter 3. b) a recruit 4. c) aria
5. c) a vassal 6. d) starling 7. c) NASA 8. d) Spanish
9. c) Spanish 10. b) Egypt

Game #23
1. d) curling 2. b) an escalator 3. c) a tripod 4. c) meteor
5. d) Missouri 6. b) a bridge 7. d) spinach 8. a) *It Takes Two*
9. c) hibernate 10. d) harp

Game #24
1. c) Tarsus 2. b) brimstone 3. b) Friday 4. a) medal 5. b) lecture
6. b) enamel 7. c) tantrum 8. d) decade
9. b) Louis XIV and Philippe 10. c) Saudi Arabia

Game #25
1. a) a stage set 2. b) school grounds 3. d) vicar 4. d) zoology
5. c) linoleum 6. d) a Dubliner 7. a) a phonograph
8. a) Kenan and Kel 9. c) Edgar Allan Poe 10. d) cudgel

Game #26
1. b) New Hampshire 2. d) a dog 3. c) sailor
4. a) a lantern 5. c) eye 6. a) Jove 7. b) ceramist
8. d) animals 9. b) Lent 10. b) ears

Game #27
1. d) AFL 2. d) Boston 3. c) botany 4. b) Mark Twain
5. d) anxious 6. b) a fleece 7. d) torpedo 8. c) Uruguay
9. b) v-shaped 10. a) Venice, Italy

Game #28
1. a) appear 2. a) Costa Rica 3. c) *Small Soldiers* 4. b) fake
5. a) Orion 6. d) thin ice 7. a) reptiles 8. b) snowstorm
9. b) New York 10. d) zebra

Game #29
1. a) James 2. b) amphibians 3. c) German 4. a) Washington
5. b) secrets can be heard 6. d) seamstress 7. c) Vermont
8. a) Thomas Jefferson 9. b) chaplain 10. c) Caledonia

Game #30
1. b) Paris 2. b) arcade 3. c) horse 4. c) warriors
5. a) one hundred 6. d) banana 7. b) Britain 8. d) wafer
9. a) Philadelphia 10. b) The Pentagon

Game #31
1. d) U.S. Air Force Academy 2. b) pickling 3. c) Appomattox
4. d) tennis 5. a) a small bouquet 6. b) Valhalla 7. c) England
8. a) gnu 9. a) spun sugar 10. d) California

Game #32
1. a) David 2. d) catfish 3. a) an occupation 4. c) Washington
5. b) Young and the Restless 6. c) pasture 7. b) Zeus
8. b) trumpet 9. d) beanball 10. b) Utah

Game #33
1. a) Bulgaria 2. c) Diana 3. a) Thurman Munson 4. d) Portug
5. b) mizzenmast 6. d) dimension 7. b) in a museum
8. a) the deck 9. d) *Days of Our Lives* 10. c) Ike

Game #34
1. b) infantile paralysis 2. b) Spiker and Sponge 3. a) the crew
4. a) Nero 5. b) Liesel Matthews 6. c) Hank Gowdy 7. c) tapest
8. b) Brenda 9. a) Sarah Michelle Gellar 10. a) Poor Richard

Game #35
1. b) "Bad Boys" 2. c) a burr 3. d) Paris 4. b) Barker
5. c) gardenia 6. a) a jacket 7. c) Ty Cobb 8. c) Bill Cosby
9. c) troupe 10. d) fifth

Game #36
1. a) Hebrews 2. c) Beth 3. b) New Jersey 4. a) Latin
5. a) Sandy Koufax 6. b) an emergency phone 7. b) Houston
8. c) Alfred Nobel 9. c) Pittsburgh 10. d) King Arthur

Game #37
1. a) Joe DiMaggio 2. b) eloquent 3. b) Saul 4. a) doe
5. c) Belgium 6. d) Hawaii 7. c) alloy 8. b) Guglielmo Marconi
9. c) Egypt 10. a) a signature

Game #38
1. d) Michigan 2. a) a duplicator 3. a) a magnetic mineral
4. b) a singer 5. c) an eyeglass 6. b) shallow
7. b) "Gold and silver" 8. a) Corsica 9. a) neurology 10. c) Canada

Game #39
1. d) Thomas Alva Edison 2. a) Kate Winslet in Titanic
3. b) a presidential hideaway 4. a) Louis XIV
5. a) *Diagnosis Murder* 6. b) patent 7. b) Napoleon Bonaparte
8. b) Nigeria 9. a) Davis 10. a) stretch

Game #40
1. b) limited monarchy 2. c) upbeat 3. c) substantive
4. c) Bismarck, ND 5. b) digit 6. a) farrier 7. b) *Billy Madison*
8. c) hint 9. b) first cousins 10. c) graph

Game #41
1. a) a livestock enclosure 2. d) make hats 3. a) god of mischief
4. d) metronome 5. d) Eritrea 6. c) Virginia 7. c) uranium
8. a) spelling 9. c) *Carmen* 10. a) franking

Game #42
1. a) *Space Jam* 2. b) Turkey 3. c) control 4. c) suburbs
5. a) Gaelic 6. c) the brig 7. d) mouth 8. c) Panama Canal
9. a) Saturn 10. b) Gettysburg

Game #43
1. c) Jim Tobin 2. a) a crook 3. c) Peru 4. d) Seminole 5. d) Venu
6. c) Louisiana 7. a) control panel 8. a) fashionable 9. c) bed
10. c) Julia Roberts

Game #44
1. b) Ganges 2. c) Eleanor 3. b) Saladin 4. d) tide 5. b) two week
6. b) a fruit 7. b) Custer 8. d) Albanian 9. a) Columbia
10. d) Shazam

Game #45
1. b) Caitlin 2. b) Norway 3. c) South Carolina 4. a) bullpen
5. b) Inuit 6. c) celeste 7. b) cygnet 8. c) Switzerland
9. a) three horns 10. a) Jane

Game #46
1. a) *10 Things I Hate About You* 2. b) South Dakota 3. b) Englan
4. c) four 5. b) a census 6. b) chinaware 7. d) Portugal
8. c) a pyramid 9. b) India 10. c) a shrimp

Game #47
1. c) Kevin McHale 2. c) French 3. d) accountant
4. b) Wednesday 5. d) Russia 6. b) Canada 7. c) Herbert Hoove
8. c) tiger 9. b) Oviraptors 10. c) Deborah

Game #48
1. a) Alberta 2. a) pit bull 3. c) Yosemite 4. c) shoulder
5. d) Spaniards and Mexicans 6. b) orbit 7. c) Hernando Corte
8. c) Hartford 9. d) Venus 10. b) Atlantis

Game #49
1. b) a shredder 2. a) Quito 3. a) Airedale 4. a) a battleship
5. c) Mindanao 6. a) a cab driver 7. b) Medus
8. c) Protoceratops 9. b) an automobile
10. a) Sandra Day O'Connor

Game #50
1. d) coroner 2. c) Jezebel 3. b) enlisting 4. c) femur
5. c) cub 6. a) Punch 7. b) Flag Day 8. d) bark
9. c) John F. Kennedy 10. c) biography

Game #51
1. d) unicorn 2. c) lettuce 3. c) personal identification 4. d) Indiana
5. d) termite 6. a) Iowa 7. b) Iran 8. c) Ireland 9. b) Komodo
10. a) crime

Game #52
1. d) thirty-two 2. c) print-makers 3. a) a plum 4. d) handball
5. c) Japanese 6. b) Mr. Hyde 7. d) Kansas 8. c) Nepal
9. c) tympani 10. b) a pirate

Game #53
1. c) *Wind in the Willows* 2. c) nectar and ambrosia 3. d) Venus
4. a) fossil dinosaur eggs 5. a) The Argonauts 6. a) Finland
7. c) Revolutionary War 8. c) Hercules 9. d) airplane flight
10. d) China

Game #54
1. c) Alexander the Great 2. d) Madame Butterfly 3. c) bowling
4. b) an insect 5. c) Brooklyn 6. b) Scotland 7. c) a riot
8. a) Helena, MT 9. b) Russian conquerors
10. c) the Sandwich Islands

Game #55

1. c) a marshy region 2. b) Hong Kong 3. c) New York City
4. d) a brogue 5. b) Washington, DC 6. c) Spain
7. b) a French palace and forest 8. c) Nepal 9. c) Dutch auction
10. b) Austria-Hungary

Game #56

1. a) being absent without leave 2. a) Pacific coast
3. c) near Colorado Springs 4. b) The Netherlands 5. c) Esau's
6. a) The Hambletonian 7. c) France 8. b) Hamelin
9. d) West Virginia 10. c) Gaul

Game #57

1. c) "Marching Through Georgia" 2. a) Ellis Island 3. c) German
4. d) no place 5. b) Britain 6. a) a British boys school
7. a) Glasgow, Scotland 8. b) W. G. Fargo of Wells Fargo
9. c) Goa 10. b) scaffold

Game #58

1. d) mercury 2. c) Alaska 3. a) Styx 4. b) Olympus 5. b) surveyor
6. d) Skye 7. c) Iowa 8. c) 1850-1870 9. a) Staffordshire
10. d) stump

Game #59

1. d) bovine 2. b) Point Barrow, Alaska 3. b) an amphibian
4. d) Vanderbilt 5. c) Vermont 6. b) he won two Nobel Prizes
7. b) Buffy 8. a) Wight 9. d) Minnesota 10. b) India

Game #60

1. b) mallet 2. a) oil 3. b) Jupiter 4. a) curling 5. b) Hot Springs, AR
6. a) Port Charles 7. c) acetylsalicylic acid 8. d) Great Britain
9. b) lions 10. c) Benjamin Franklin